MW00523134

Happy life!
Maryanne Barnes

A Cat is Better Than a Boyfriend

EXCEPT
FOR THE SEX

WRITTEN BY: MARYANNE BARNES
INSPIRED BY: THE CAT MORGAN

A RELATIONSHIP TAIL OF TWO FRIENDS

Published by

K Y O D A I & C O M P A N Y
S A N   F R A N C I S C O

C o p y r i g h t   2 0 1 0

All rights reserved
including the right of reproduction
in whole or in part in any form.

Printed in the USA
ISBN 978-0-578-04949-6

realize the value
of unconditional love

my son, in a nesting mode.

Thirty-five, single, and falling in love with model types who just don't want the "house full of little Andrews" that he wants. So, on a routine run in Golden Gate Park near his San Francisco place, he passed this cat all alone alongside the path. Finishing the 5-mile run the cat was still there and alone.

Remember his "nesting mode," …

So he took it home and 2 weeks later it delivered 3 kittens.

The SPCA in San Francisco is wonderful!

Not aggressively pro-animal, anti-people place. They send you a video on cat care, advice on various kinds of kitty litter, types of cat food, and answer phone questions all the time.

A life-saver for the new dad.

I knew dada about cats.

Two and a half

months later, my son asked if I wanted
the black & white kitten from the litter.
He would keep mother cat and the brown and white kitten
(because the colors matched his furniture) as company for each other.
His roofer took the black kitten for his son.

I declined the offer, saying I knew nothing about cats and, really, did
not like them. Then at three months Andy phoned again and sounded
like he was offering his child to me. What choice did I have - I had
to say yes. So I bought Andy a plane ticket and he paid a $100 animal
fee to fly to Pittsburgh. Imagine sitting five hours in the last-row, up-
right seat with the cage right on the floor under his bent knees!

Just a mention, not a complaint.

The Cat Room

Andy's spacious three-bedroom apartment was on the third floor of a San Francisco apartment building. Large rooms, rooftop porch with a bench and lots of potted plants, making a safe haven for Mother Cat and her three newborn kittens.

One bedroom became The Cat Room complete with litter box, pink rubber litter pad in the shape of a cat's face, toys of all colors to roll or dangle or just play with, food, water and organic wheat greens. Mother Cat liked the clothes closet best and she and her kittens lived there 3 months. The SPCA advised Andy to play with mother cat 20 minutes every day. Being a first time father, Andy complied and after playtime, Mother Cat was happy and retreated to the clothes closet in The Cat Room. The place was quiet all day every day because Andy was at work, went to happy hours, still ran his 5 miles around Golden Gate Park. Weekends were busy away from home, too.

I think that's why my kitten came to me super-shy.

Baby

Morgan thought I was her Mother.

Computer ~ on my lap,
reading the newspaper ~ my lap.

I had no idea how to get away.

Every time I sat down, Morgan wanted

on my

lap.

Who's smiling now?

"Trader Joe's humorous go at uppity"

Trader Joe's in Pittsburgh is in a rough part of town now an "urban redevelopment" block. It has an air-of-superiority customers, traces of humor in their signage and labels.

Driving past one day I stopped in.

Kiwi fruit drink, soy milk, inexpensive tofu, free coffee of the day, sampling beautiful corn squash. For my Cat, I sought cat food, turned out to be something uppity. The aisles are slim so a shopper cannot ponder. I looked up and down and found it!

A big smile on my face and an out loud "look at this."

There it was, cat food, named HOLISTIC NATURAL FELINE FORMULA. I have been reusing that good-looking container for the usual Science Diet stuff for a great smile at morning feedings.

Who's smiling more now ~ Cat or me?

A little
adventure
never hurt
anyone.

About treats

Like my wanting something special after a long day at work,
I give Cat an organic treat when I want her to feel special.

Once in a while the newspaper has a coupon for treats and it's fun
buying a different packet.

After all variety is the spice of life!

Recently, Jeanne visited me and brought a bag of treats. My normally
shy Cat went wild playing, rolling over with wide-eyed attention to
this visitor. Amazing. What fun!!! A little adventure never hurt
anyone.

Wonder if it was catnip or treats?

"Mysterious cats"

I open the door to the side porch and invite my Cat to go out to sit in the sunshine on the wicker chairs which are just inches from the door.

It seems Cat is considering, thinking about my request, like somehow trying to solve a built-in mysteriousness.

Not at all! A woman in my garden club, who loves cats, dogs, horses, etc, spoke up one time while on the subject, that cats' brains are the size of a pea!!

So as not to be misunderstood, I picked up the Cat and walked her outside where she sits or stretches out happily.

No miscommunication here.

Simplicity is Morgan's middle name.

My cat is not my buddy

a dog is a buddy.

It needs my words and strokes but does not play fetch or tricks
~ although I did teach the SIT command and she knows now
what to do.

Not always, however.

Love my cat's yawns.

Figure it is a "hello, look what I can do performance."

I love it and say so, then once in a while she does
it all over again.

Looking at my email today, there is an attachment from a fellow member of my Women's Business Network. She offers, "Tips for Reducing Stress." Dianafletcher.com.

"10 tips that relate to my Cat.

1 **Remember you are important** and that you deserve time for yourself. Just sitting here at my desk, I love stroking the cat at my own pace.

2 **Say yes to what brings you joy**. Just looking at the cat sleep or stretch ~ a nap isn't so bad after all.

3 **Let some things go.** The Cat claws the needlepoint seats I made while taking the kids to their doctor appointments or watching their little league games (4 kids in 6 years ~ that's a lot of needlepoint). Important and truly beautiful up to recently, but seat covers can be replaced easily. The workmanship is beautiful but it was very much the needlework experience.

4 **Drink water.** What fun to watch Morgan jump onto the bathroom sink to taste fresh faucet water while I brush my teeth and have the first glassful each day.

5 **Laugh out loud.** Watching Cat, lying on her back, playing with, aggressively swatting, the mechanical mouse swirling overhead. It has a sensor and is triggered by animal motion. Every so often, she just saunters over and plays with it. Great fun.

6 **Breathe.** Watching TV with Cat lying across my lap. Feeling it breathing gently makes me also breathe gently.

7 **Make time for yourself.** I've got a window seat where afternoon sunshine pours in. Cat stretches out there some afternoons and I just lie alongside her and catch a catnap for 10 minutes every now and then.

8 **Hug.** Often I've arrived at a meeting or event with tiny cat hairs on my shirt or jacket. Out loud I have said, "got to stop hugging Cat on my way out the door" to no one in particular.

9 **Say yes to fun!** Taking Cat to Petco's toy dept and asking the Cat to pick out something. Sounds nutso but it is a really fun to do.

10 **Tell someone you love them.** Saying " I love you" aloud is so nice. Cat lives here and makes the place noticeably happy. These happy feelings ratchet down my blood pressure.

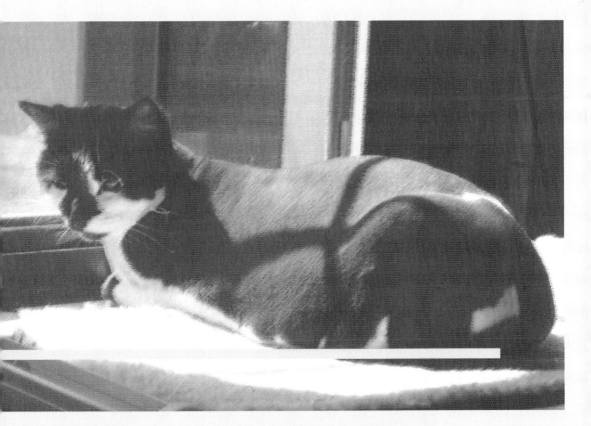

'slight' cat

No?

No known allergies up until Morgan.

She walks over my face during the night. My eyes got little attention, but when the bags under the eyes could take me on a trip, it was time to see the allergist. The allergy tests showed dust, trees and SLIGHT cat. So much for that.

I had some major surgery 3 years ago. Every hospital person passing by had to ask over and over if I were allergic to anything. My answer "I don't think so", " I don't think so", then changed to "well, my cat!" So much for that, see the hospital bracelet that hangs on my dresser mirror and makes me smile.

Pathetically funny.

Yippee

not a weird idea

About 3 years along, my condo started looking like a yarn factory.

I brush my cat at least every week because it is such a pleasure
taking care of her, but I do not vacuum all that regularly.
Small tumbleweeds were forming in corners where I do not walk.

So, let's see if I can talk a groomer into a cat buzz cut, like my son's
head when he was little. Local salon groomer said oh, sure, we have
one we do every month because its owners are allergic!

 Yippee, not a weird idea.

My cat, a 14 lb stray with shaggy hair, looked sensational in her new
hair cut as a Chihuahua with Kimba-style tail hair.

Makes me laugh out loud! (See # 5 Tips)

ready
to sleep
in her
own bed

We all need

a little vacation. From time to time Morgan stays at the Golden Bone Pet Resort. Golden Bone Pet Resort advertises 7 color TVs, healthy filtered air and exercise three times daily.

(Maybe your cat does, but most cats do not watch TV ~ their eyes move too fast and so it's blurry. TV waves have to accommodate human speed, which is slower. Nice thought, though ....)

The Resort cat room is lined with good-sized cages stacked 4 high. I send along a toy and an old nightshirt of mine for company. Just so she takes a little bit of "home" with her.

So, 3 times daily Morgan sits in the middle of the big playroom floor at the resort with lots of toys. She sits or crouches there for an hour then goes back to sleep in the cage. *Exercise?*

Here's the funny part: in my car to home she meows louder than a radio ~ like a jungle ME-OW! Guess she sees what other cats do.

Perhaps ....

she's enjoyed her vacation but is ready to sleep in her own bed.

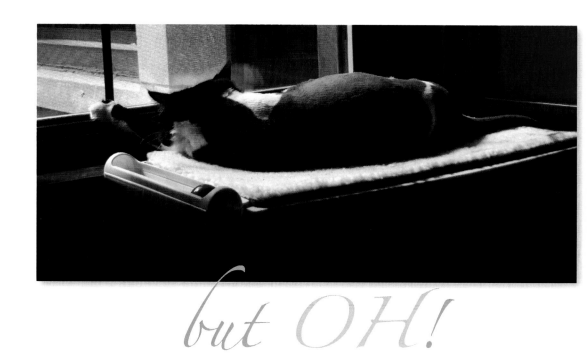

but OH!

Hissing

Morgan

had a feral parent and a "hide under the bed" personality type that has taken 6 years of my constant socialization efforts. She hides from the mailman while he's still at the end of the driveway.

I saw a cartoon where a dog wearing one of those blue medical collars said to the nearby dog that "now I can hear the mailman SIX blocks away". This describes Cat even without the collar.

My cat and I moved into a large mansion's first floor condo with lots of big windows, large windowsills and window seats. Not sure of her new home, she really stayed under the bed at first. She was shy seeing cars passing and people strolling by on the sidewalk. It is 3 years now and if she can see it and watch happenings from a distance it's OK. But if people get too close on the nearby walkway it's back to "ears up and eyes wide open" and always on guard.

In this socialization effort, I've taken her shopping for "cat food", gone on little trips and out for yearly shots. A pleasure seeing her just co-existing while looking at other dogs and mice and fish ~ they weren't a threat.

But OH, the Animal Friends caged cats for adoption along the front wall! They were just hanging out and there was Cat hissing loudly at her fellow felines.

Surprising.

Morgan exercises enough I guess

she gets carried.

Trips

Morgan exercises enough, I guess.

Cat food Science Diet does not put on the pounds but just in case,
it is my job to give a little walk now and then.

She gets carried to my assigned parking spot 200 steps away,
gets down and marches right back to my side porch and
waits under the wicker chairs for me to catch up and open the
door to go back inside.

Gives me lots of pleasure to take these 'trips' with her nearly
every day.

I get double the steps,

so am I exercising her *or is she exercising me?*

That

Day

Peeing

in the suitcase.

Do not try this at home: an open satchel invites my Cat to pee there.

She did not have an unhappy childhood and was never neglected
or hollered at or bullied or pushed around.

So I cannot figure why she has to "make a statement". Perhaps it was
the first three months in my son's clothes closet with Mother Cat and
the kittens that made Cat feel at home.

Happened two different times before I figured it out that open suitcases
invite Cat.

The worst of which was my visitor's slacks. She insisted I have
everything dry-cleaned THAT DAY. I was embarrassed and
overwhelmed to hear no same day service from every dry cleaner
I called. It did happen, however.

Like someone once said "there isn't anything you can't do
with money."

Not my quote but I think it often.

Great Smile

After

... the yearly immunizations, since it was so close to
Christmas Day, Petco had a Santa Claus for a photo, for a
small donation to the humane society.

So for $2 we have a guy with a great smile, beard that doesn't fit,
a suit terribly hot, and one scared Cat.

What fun, no?

one cat

Saint Francis

loved animals so some religions have a special annual service
where pets are invited to the church grounds for a blessing.

Sounded interesting; in talking to some friends in Atlanta,
I understand the same blessing attracts people who even bring their
horses, can you imagine?

Rev. White, pastor of St. Scholastica, blessed over 30 dogs
and one cat, Morgan.

*Relaxed
and in control.*

Relationships

Healthy relationships allow us to maintain
a sense of who we are and what we're all about.

Each of us makes choices about what will make us happy,
how important it is to become your own person
and not depend on others to define you.

Unconditional love from either boyfriend or cat ~ accepting us for our
strengths and weaknesses, but love just the same, is priceless.

Find your joy, set time aside to smell the flowers

hug someone,

or a Cat,

YOU love.

Maryanne Barnes

I love my life

About the Author

Maryanne Barnes is an accomplished businesswoman that realizes the value of unconditional love. She has won numerous business awards and served on a variety of boards. A longtime member of Woodland Garden Club, Maryanne fills her spirit learning about flowers and plants.

"Staying happy is genes plus work (with or without pay) in this great Country with countless opportunities. The answer to Happiness is thinking you are in control of your life, no matter what you do."

Four grown sons, each a winner, influenced by a Mom who taught the pleasure of making your own living by work.

"I love my life, my home, flowers, being in the sunshine, relaxing with Morgan the Cat, and sometimes a glass of Shiraz."

True happiness ... multiple relationships, friends, family, boyfriends and yes ... even a cat!

Dear Reader,
Your thoughts …